# *Rhythm and Life*

## *A Poetry Anthology*

## *by*

## *Vaughan Stone*

# Contents

# Contents *(continued)*

## Faith

## Fun

# Sussex

# Swan Lake

I lose myself in beauty at the edge of Hove lagoon
As swans glide by with easy grace and unselfconscious pride,
Ignoring all the raucous cries of that intense platoon
Of herring-gulls that cluster beak to beak along the side.
The cob spikes up his glistening quills to catch the morning rays,
His neck looped back to balance all that thrusting, surging

power;

The pen, serene, her neck stretched up, now languidly surveys
The paradise around her, stooping only to devour
The weed below the surface or the soggy bread afloat –
The kindly gift of mothers wheeling infants round the lake;
The lazy flap of canvas as the youngsters sail their boat,
Unconscious of the splintered sunlight shining from their wake;
The muted roar of distant trucks, reluctant to intrude
Upon the healing touch of fringe-of-earshot solitude.
The swaying dancers revel in the sparkling joy of June –
There never was a ballet like the one on Hove lagoon.

# Newtimber Hill

The Weald was choked in clinging murk,
The Downs stretched up, the chalky steep
Submerged in swathes of miry clay;
The trees like ghosts about my path
Let fall their droplets in my hair.
The muggy air was breathless, still,
As I climbed upward swathed in gloom;
The deadened silence wrapped me round,
No sound from birds too glum to sing.

I slithered on the slippery slope,
Then climbed the stile and left the wood
To feel my mood to lighten some.
The mist still clung to sodden grass
As I resumed my weary climb.
But suddenly the gloom was gone
And sunshine bathed the landscape, while
The golden gorse was scattered wide
And spiders strung their diamonds there.

(Cont'd)

The sky stretched round in deepest blue
With larks ecstatic, hovering there.
I revelled in this fairyland.
Below, the tower of Poynings church
Just pierced the clouds that hid the nave,
Reminder of the certain hope
That lifts the soul beyond the tomb
And out into the sunlight, where
The fresher air excites the breath.

Winter and Spring have hastened by
And Summer still extends its reign
As I climb nimbly through the shade.
The Weald below is bright and clear
And Wolstanbury bathes in light
As does the hill to westward, which
Is cleft in two by Devil's Dyke.
Silence, peace, relaxing space –
My favourite place, Newtimber Hill.

# High Tide at Hove

A line of sentinels stands guard along the shore
An inch above the highest reaches of the tide
And poised to swoop.
The waters with a gentle swish subside
Beyond the rattling shingle, and before
They can regroup
The gulls flap down with raucous screech
To raid the cockles and the crabs.
More cautious, crows descend the beach
To seize whatever's up for grabs.

The merest hint of waves returning from retreat –
Enough to scare the crows to hurry back to where
They stood before,
Abandoning the feast; they do not dare
To let the surf-topped wavelets wash their feet
Or cleanse a claw.
The gulls are not so timid and
Remain to scavenge there until
They too no longer can withstand
The undertow and overspill.

They wait with patience as their larder is restocked;
The pulsing sea withdraws and leaves the door unlocked.

# *Nature*

# Theme With Variations

The day goes racing by and has its fling,
The nightingale enchants the shortening nights
As April leaves; the bluebell wood delights
The eye as longer days bring on the Spring.
A theme with variations.

The day full-grown; the night in full retreat
As swifts and martins revel in the light
With swooping, soaring fantasies of flight,
And poppies flash their joy from fields of wheat.
A theme with variations.

The rhythm of the year hems in the day,
The lazy sun shakes slumber from his eye
To light the diamond webs; while in the sky
The swallows gather, risking no delay.
A theme with variations.

The night encroaches; daylight fast foreclosed
As Winter flaunts his talons to the stark
Bare landscape; while so secret in the dark
The plant-cells are dividing. Who composed
This theme with variations?

# The Forest

The stillness of the Highlands winter night
Seeps into every corner of the mind,
The shadowed snow beneath the trees combined
With twilight to evoke that mystic white.
The pines exude their tang while standing black
Against the sky, their scattered needles strewn
Beneath them as they aid the rising moon
To paint her zebra-stripes across the track.
A browsing stag appears without a sound,
His antlers brushing off a gentle shower
To ruffle so the silence of the hour,
And stamps his twinned impressions in the ground.
The dormant buds that clothe the naked larch
Prepare in secret for the end of March.

# Day And Night

Reluctant the day to emerge from the mist
That clings to the earth in a tender embrace
Until the proud sun gently comes to insist
And insist – that his sunbeams be given a place
To light up the frost in a dazzling display
And welcome with joy the return of the day.

Revealed is the lace of the webmaster's skill
A-sparkle with rainbows. The shadows withdraw,
The frost turns to tears and surrenders its chill
Succumbing so slowly, reluctant to thaw.
Still is the air while caressing the cheek,
As dawn remains loath to yield up its mystique.

Majestic, the sun climbs asserting his right,
Steadfastly confident, claiming his throne,
Scattering colour, assurance, delight,
Comforting warmth on the shoulders; the drone
Of late-searching bees in these shortening days
Making the most of those sovereign rays.

(*Cont'd*)

Berries flash scarlet in random design
As lazily passes the languorous day,
Succulent fruit swelling ripe on the vine
And roses providing a haunting display
To gladden the eye while bewitching the nose
As afternoon grudgingly draws to its close.

Rapidly now sinks the sun to the west,
Twilight lays fingers so cool on the face,
Bats flicker silently by on their quest
For gnats on the wing, while the very last trace
Of sunset fades gracefully, gently from sight
To welcome the silence and peace of the night.

Cold constellations invade the cold sky;
Frost spreads its tentacles, crisping the lawn;
The owl rends the night with his shivering cry,
While earth is awaiting the soft scent of dawn
And darkness tries valiantly still to persist.
Reluctant the day to emerge from the mist.

# Waves

Surrounding us each moment of the day
And of the night, those silent radio waves,
Invisible and clothed in mystery –
But true!
Those other waves that dance beyond the spectrum,
Caress with soothing fingers to bring healing
With content
And relaxation if in gentle doses,
But full of menace if untamed by oceans
Of ozone.

The gentle lapping of the waves upon the beach
Seems more in tune to touch our understanding
And summon feelings of security
And blessed peace.
But violent walls of water summoned up
By cataclysms deep beneath the sea
And far away,
Can smash their way in devastating might
Through unaware communities. We fail
To understand.

*(Cont'd)*

Humanity's desire to circumvent
Disasters of this kind, will gladly take
The willing hand of science to protect its legacy.
That willing hand already has devised
The way to trap and harness those long rays
Of infra-red;
But why so long to overcome the snags
In mastering the force of wave and tide
For energy?

Let us then enjoy the tingling touch
Of morning sun as he so gently strokes
Those sensual receptors on the back and shoulders.
Take time to listen to the patient pulse
Of wavelets as they happily seduce
The shingled shore.
Let us revel *now* in all the beauty
And the wonder of this vast creation
We fear to lose.

# Daydreaming

A grassy bank beneath, I close my eyes
For wishful thinking to possess my mind;
Those thoughts will wing their way and seek to find
Some glimpses of a far-off paradise.
A cruise through sunny Caribbean seas?
The scent of roasting chestnuts by the fire?
Fulfilment of the lover's deep desire?
Recapture of those childhood memories?
Now free of tension, all my muscles ease,
Caressed by thoughts of southern sunlit sands
And quivering thrill of fantasy romance
As naked skin is tickled by the breeze.
My eyelids open – now the dream comes true;
The sky above is deepest sapphire blue...

# Dewdrops

They glitter at the touch of morning sun
And sparkle as the zephyrs brush the grass
Or heedless insects ruffle it and pass
Upon their way; the diamonds one by one
Trans-twinkled as the sun dispels the mist,
To emerald or ruby – then a switch
To sapphire as the golden rays bewitch
The mind, and change the gems to amethyst.
A twitching of the eye seems to deflect
The magic beams, revealing polished gold,
Encouraging the spirit to reflect
And watch the beauty of the day unfold.
By noon the sun decides he will withdraw
Those jewels and restock his treasure-store.

# Skyscape

Those snow-flanked mountains of the stratosphere
That sit so snug on the horizon's rim
And glide so gently, softly disappear,
Obedient to the wind's despotic whim.
They leave a backdrop of the deepest blue
Until that unseen stagehand shuffles on
A further cordillera passing through
Which fills the vision till it too is gone.
The threat of nimbus dims the lights
And apprehension fills the viewers' gaze;
The crack of thunder and the flash excites
Full-blooded fear at such intense displays.
The lights switch on, the sun accepts his cue
And all the stage is bathed again in blue.

# Garden Gait

Sparrows all a-twitter and a-flutter and a-scurry,
Scuttling at random, playing 'tag' among the leaves,
Never flagging, never still.

Arrogant, jaunty, ungainly, uncouth,
Swaggering, lurching, the starlings invade
Jerking and strutting en masse.

Woodpigeon, belly all a-flopping as he waddles
Neck a-jerking, anxious, unselfconscious as he toddles;
Gobbles up the seeds along the path.

Not so ungainly, the dove ambles gently
Softly advancing with self-conscious glance
Over her shoulder, advancing with care.

Hop.... hop.... run straight ahead;
Pause.. canter.... stop.... cock an ear.
*Ad hoc* meal for the blackbird!

Jumping lightly from the handle of the spade
The robin bobs and bustles as he pounces,
Sprightly bouncing back to his perch.

Here a peck, there a peck, hopping in from nowhere,
Dunnocks, shy as ever, hug the edges of the lawn.
Ducking where the hedge is..... Now they are gone!

# Home

# The Miracle

I gaze in wonder at the evidence
Of life curled up within that hidden womb,
And marvel at the hope it represents
Of latent love, beloved and soon to bloom;
To realize the integrated maze
Of nerves and arteries minutely planned,
Of waterways and food canals in phase
And patient airways waiting to expand!
That pair of hearts in harmony pulsating
A lullaby of soothing, gentle thunder
Will reassure until the time of waiting
Erupts into the breathless joy and wonder
Of life evolved. What marvel to be seeing
A soul, a *person* so loved into *being*.

(*The last two lines completed on 14.03.2006,
the day after my grandson's birth*)

# Persian Princess

She was a tiny trembling ball of fluff
But now full-grown and of the royal line.
The tingling touch of Persian silk enough
To shiver its delight along my spine.
The loud ecstatic rumble of her purring
Vibrates along the surface of my thighs
Until I need to shuffle, thus incurring
Reproach made clear from scandal-widened eyes.
Forgiven, now I feel her nuzzling jaw
Transmit affection to my willing cheek,
And then the rhythmic clutch of paw and claw
In well-rehearsed though damaging technique.
A rule of nature not to be forgotten,
That love can only be by love begotten.

# Grateful Warmth

Tender the flame as the match touches tinder,
Hesitant shyly to challenge the dark;
Scarcely a shiver resisting the winter,
Just a faint quiver of hope from the spark.
Suddenly shooting from under the starkness
Of splinters and twigs, come the roar and the blaze.
Flaming, the fangs that devour the darkness
Revel in brash adolescent displays.
Now imperceptibly, ardour subsiding,
Steady the heat and more adult the flame,
Comfort and cheer relaxation providing,
Flickered reflection the name of the game.
Stillness and peace are the gems to remember
As embers now greet the demise of November.

# Mind

# Me

Strange is the concept of such a small word!
Is it so simple to understand 'me'?
What image conjures up when it is heard?
How complicated the meaning – 'to be'!
What is my identity?

Is it just the wrinkles on my forehead,
The twinkle that might sometimes light my eyes?
Stumbling gait that sometimes has me worried,
Or other traits that people recognize?
Is that my identity?

All of that is really so subjective –
My fingerprints are what the Law desires.
DNA is really more effective
To counteract the fairy-tales of liars.
That proves my identity?

DNA is certainly objective
But fails to bring to light the hidden 'me';
Memories, emotions, hope's perspective
Are buried in the mind's obscurity.
Are they my identity?

(Cont'd)

Deeper than heredity's formation
And all the human foibles that men see,
Real self is God's direct creation –
The specialized uniqueness that is me.
That is my identity.

# The Grey and the Blue

Smothered by a cloud of pointlessness
And choked by twists of undefined despair,
Bright colours dulled;
The day is new but full of emptiness
And evening seems so distant, ushering in
A lonely night.

Days drag by while years seem fleeting.
Conscience nags, remorse bites deep
For chances missed;
Decay, old age and death may seem to blur
Perception of reality; the senses
Swamped by grey.

How to struggle free of such depression?
Where to find awareness, find the key
To liberty?
Beyond the stifling grey, the blue is real
The sun is there; and what if space beyond
Be wrapped in love?

(Cont'd)

Bright-coloured flowers are real – false the pastel,
The empty day is waiting to be filled
With dazzling hope,
And just as 'blue' is real above the stratus,
So Life, while blossoming beyond the grave,
Expels despair.

Maybe the clouds are there, but only passing;
Hope and promise – they are real
Beyond the gloom,
Witnessed by the joy of Easter.
Death, decay, old age defeated –
Empty tomb!

# *Away With Depression*

The dreary sound of drumming rain
And weary chill of winter's blast
Seem like a never-ending chain
That binds the present to the past.
The spirit sags beneath the strain
And makes the listless body wilt,
Geared to an apathetic brain.
But wait! A life can yet be built
As Spring brings on another day,
While cheerful birds delay their rest
In happy hope that they may lay
Those precious eggs within the nest.
So humankind is richly blest –
There is no call to be depressed.

# Fresh Voices

Deaf he was from out the very womb,
A mystery those moving lips;
Messages transferred without a sound.
But what was silence? What was sound?
Just meaningless abstractions that
He'd pondered.

No voices had intruded on his mind
Until the exultation of that day
When those vibrations first could penetrate
The labyrinthine channels of the ear,
So bring the choking wonderment of sound
And hearing.

The creaking trolleys and the rustling sheets,
The sound of laughter and the jig-saw mix
Of alien speech with clouded meaning;
Whispers, groans, the splash of tea,
Twanging mattress-springs –
And clatter.

How strange to him that those unfelt vibrations
Had flowed insistently within his ears
Unheeded, wholly lost to his perception
Quite undetected through those passing years,
Excluded by the lack of a receptor
Until now.

No stranger than those other subtle voices
That whirl around our unresponsive head,
Unceasing waves that swiftly pass unnoticed,
Anonymous, elusive; out of reach
Until the touching of a switch can make
A capture.

So are there wonders still to be discovered?
Fresh voices yet that struggle to be heard
And cherished in the mind and in the silence?
Soft messages of love from distant shores,
Fresh whispers brought by pathways
Yet unknown?

And how can we detect such unknown voices
So bathing in the warmth they might inspire?
What wizardry might bring to our perceiving
The rich reality that far beyond
Is someone, known or stranger,
One who cares?

# Light

The greatest mystery the Universe displays –
And hides! The light.
It bathes our vision daily with its secret rays.
The stars shine white,
Bewitching with the view of how decades ago
They scattered beams that only reach us here below
Tonight.

The greatest challenge to mankind is to unravel
Strands of thought;
To understand the means by which the sunbeams travel
To be brought
Those ninety million miles, unveiling all the glory
Night had hidden; explanation of the story
Longtime sought.

Are there really waves that bring the beauty of the dawn
To light our eyes?
Or is that joyful gift by particles so tiny borne –
Truth in disguise?
Can both these teasing mysteries in harmony exist?
This paradox is surely not so easily dismissed
As mere surmise.

More casual realities we daily take for granted
Passing by,
As rays (or particles?) impinge upon that screen implanted
In the eye,
To be transmuted by a further magic switch
To pulses in the nervous pathways which
The brain supply.

The chain of mystery is hardly then complete
But teases yet,
Confounding every vestige of humanity's conceit –
Apt to forget
That vision, sight, awareness still remain
Unanswered by the fancy networks of the brain
Together met.

God said, "Let there be light!" – and light became –
Life's mystic key!
"I am the Light," Lord Jesus would proclaim,
That man might see
That Way, that Life of love – for all mankind,
A parable for Truth to heal the blind.
Reality!

# Twist of Time

Imprisoned in the deep caves of our being
Is the concept
That Time is straight and leads us on directly
Along the trail from 'Past' to 'Now' to 'Future',
With past and future moving ever further
From each other.

But what if that is just a flawed perception
Trapping all mankind,
Disguising how the flow of Time winds onwards
And brings us in a spiral, ever closer
To cherished memories now half-forgotten?
Anniversaries?

So maybe, as the future swiftly twirls us
Round the spiral,
We shall be able to review this morning
Close up – if joy and wonder flood the present;
If not, we could delay our glance, avoiding
Painful memories.

Again, perhaps we might succeed in changing
The spiral's pitch,
Enabling us to visit those millennia
Ahead or in the past – or just tomorrow –
And catch maybe a joyful glimpse of where
The spiral ends?

# *Teasing Time*

Assumption is that Time will flow directly,
Arrow-straight to future from the past
And like a woven cord, quite undivided
Connecting up eternity with 'now'.

But could it be that Time is not continuous,
More like a beaded necklace than a cord,
Its pulses far too fast to be apparent
Like flashing frames of cinematograph?

And what might fill the gaps within that necklace?
A whole existence, separate from Time
But sharing space; could this be truly Heaven,
So close entwined with life upon the earth?

If so, the mystics surely taught correctly
That undiscovered Heaven wraps us round
And God is close, whatever our perception –
A cause for wonder, confidence and hope.

# War and Peace

The unresolved dilemma of the pacifist
When evil's recognized:
"How can I love my enemy and yet resist
His hatred realized?
How can I stand aside in apathy
And watch his victims in their agony
Be brutalized?"

The caring mind is tortured by the flow
Of arguments sincerely posed;
Can peace be honoured if the conscience know
Of bombs and tears, and lives foreclosed?
Or will the hatred gendered by a victory
Go on to fester in the latent memory
Of vanquished foe?

What chance is there that raging tyrants might defer
To love's appeal?
Can miracles be forged by love and so confer
The chance to heal?
Or will the deadly threat of bristling weaponry
Bring peace, and so postpone the bitter misery
And strike a deal?

# Relaxation

Body tensed, the muscles stretched;
Mind, obsessed with hastening Time,
Never lets the spirit rest –
Minutes wasted, heinous crime!
How can I relax?
Stop!

Let that hoarded breath escape
In a long delicious sigh;
Shoulders sag, relax the nape,
Sinews of the back untie.
Do I feel relaxed?
Yes?

Is my mouth still racked with stress?
Clenched the jaw, coiled up the tongue.
Can I really decompress
A throat that's highly overstrung?
Just collapse!
Well?

Don't let Time resume its nagging,
Banish any vain regret,
Keep the spirit far from flagging,
Don't let tension make me fret.
Can I keep relaxed?
Ah!

(Cont'd)

Now enjoy the tranquil bliss,
Revel in the mental calm,
Feel the silence plant a kiss,
Peace of mind exert its charm.
Now I feel relaxed.
Wow!

# Silence

I feel the silence softly close around me
And seep into the crannies of the heart,
Encouraging that inner relaxation,
The gentle calm for muscles, mind and self.

Awareness of the sounds of daily living
Persists, although forbidden to encroach
Upon the stillness of my own oasis
Where Time no longer nags, but peace pervades.

The sound of silence now vibrates within me
In tune with deeper longings of the soul,
And silent voices filter in from nowhere
To link me up with wider life beyond.

Where to find such paradise of silence,
Such peace to take possession deep within?
The hillside? By the waters? At the fireside?
The garden? ... or the cramped commuter train?

Can silence really be so strong, exclusive?
Tomorrow's rush-hour may provide the test.

# Faith

# Dawn of Hope

Auras of fear ring the shoulder of each
When stealthily summoned to share that last meal;
Anxious the glances, precluding all speech,
Expectant yet dreading what He might reveal.
Tenderly shared are the wine and the bread –
But scarce an hour later the diners are fled.
Overwhelmed by trepidation!

Stricken the shepherd, the sheep are all scattered;
Ridden with guilt are the claims of the brave.
All protestations of courage are shattered,
Each fears the shadow of scaffold and grave.
One lonely figure skulks far in the rear,
Trembling, remorseful and gutted with fear.
Peter, locked in isolation.

Huddled there in mournful silence
Each avoids the others' glance,
Scared themselves to suffer violence
From the hate that law demands.
Hard the guilt and grief to bear,
Shot right through with dull despair.
Gnawing, aching desolation.

(Cont'd)

Cool the morning, still the air,
Scent of spices, empty tomb;
Hope revives to oust despair,
Doubt is fading, faith in bloom.
Wonder, joy dissolve the dread –
Christ is risen from the dead!
Death's defeat, Love's vindication.

# Easter

They ran, they ran. Of course they ran
Though little need there was for haste –
The Lord was dead.
Peter, out of breath, began
To fall behind, by John outpaced.
What had they said?

What had they said, those women, when
They'd hastened back with spice unused –
An empty tomb?
They surely must have been confused,
Hope ousting truth, that hope might then
Dispel the gloom.

Filled with fear and crouched in awe
John peered but failed to penetrate
The shrouding veil,
But Peter entered, dimly saw
The linen clothes to validate
The women's tale.

Emerging to the misty morning
They looked each other in the eyes,
Doubt slowly dwindling.
Just then the sun began to rise,
A day of wonder slowly dawning,
Hope rekindling.

*(Cont'd)*

Doubt returned as night, descending,
Locked the door and saw them cower,
Gripped by fear.
Then a burst of joy transcending
All the darkness of the hour.
"The Lord is here!"

# Reality

Tranquil the ripples that tickle the sand
Wood smoke ascending to welcome the day
Fishing a peaceful activity.
Aroma of succulent fish from the strand,
Comfort of friendship to lighten the way;
Present serenity.

Three times repeated, that searching request,
"Do you now love me?" All Peter's denials
Past history.
Then the commission so gently expressed,
"Look to my flock" – and so love reconciles.
Future ministry.

Hope and compassion and strength in vocation,
Service in leadership – that is the call;
Trust in adversity.
Faith that dissolves away all trepidation
Joyfully triumphing over it all.
Heaven's reality.

# *Survival*

Restating the truth that our bodies must surely decay
To be lost to the grave and recycled, sounds terribly trite;
But truth remains truth when those dangers encroach and despite
Any lust for survival, which only gives hope of delay.
Is Truth then so morbid? Has Nature no promise to show?
Is rebirth so fanciful? No indication to lead
To glimmers of hope? Can the tiniest, tiniest seed
Not inspire us to faith with its preconceived promise to grow?
A drab-looking larva crawls out of the water to die;
It shrivels and hardens, lies still and is seemingly dead,
But all of a sudden the crust splits apart and is shed
Revealing the dragonfly's splendour, bewitching the eye.
The message it leaves by this dazzling, entrancing revival
Reminds us that we too inherit the gift of survival.

# *Trust*

Deceivers, tricksters blossom everywhere,
So surely it is foolishness to trust?
The con-men drive us daily to despair
And make us feel that life is so unjust.

Who is worthy of my trust?
Can we put our trust in one another?
The pilot or the driver of the train?
Government? Beloved? Friend or mother?
Or should we fail to trust, and just complain?
Life is empty, lacking trust.

As days go by, with little thought we trust
Familiar things and people – chairs and roof,
The surgeon and the driver, for we must
Rely upon their skill while lacking proof.
Surely they demand our trust?

Trust demands no proof – though common-sense
Is not to be despised – for such a jewel
Is offered free, devoid of all pretence
For daily, everlasting, glad renewal.
Where then might I place my trust?

(Cont'd)

"Believe in God; believe also in me" –
That's what He said. Relax into His care
And trust Him now and through eternity,
Safe wrapped within His love, and be aware
That love like this is safety.

# Truth

What is Truth? The question echoes down the years
From long before the Governor expressed
That terse request.
Is Truth for us but limited to what appears?
And should we really be obsessed
With proof and test?

Must Truth therefore remain forever undisclosed
And lurk beyond the bounds of human thought
And human vision?
Is there no answer to the question Pilate posed –
The questing mind forever to be caught
In indecision?

Reality quite independent of belief
Or unbelief, and free from what is felt or taught
Or ill-perceived;
Untrammelled by the crests and troughs of joy or grief,
Nor by the heavy intellectual report
By man conceived.

We glory in the snippets of the Truth we can discern
From here within the limits of our mortal cage,
And stretch afar
To push away the bars of ignorance, and learn
A little more to let our finite minds engage
The furthest star.

(Cont'd)

It must be right to probe and probe the mystery
Enfolding Truth, not daunted from enquiring
Through futility;
But each advance repeats the lessons of our history
That ignorance extends still faster, thus requiring
Our humility.

# Were You There?

Were you among that great ecstatic crowd
That waved their palms and welcomed the Messiah?
How disenchanted were you when you saw
That limp, dejected figure on the Cross?
Did you feel shame that you had been deceived;
Awareness that you too had been betrayed?
And later, when the rumours spread abroad
Of resurrection, did you shrink away
Refusing to be conned a second time?

His closest friends had failed to recognize
The flesh renewed. So was there something else
To recognize – that inward real self
That radiates its life from deep within?
Was that how finally they recognized
Their friend, and so renewed their fractured faith?
If so, perhaps you too can realize
His presence, and regain your shattered hope.

# To Welcome a Stranger

To Canterbury, far from distant Rome
He came to bring good news to heathen folk.
We made him welcome in our island home
Prepared to shelter underneath his cloak
And welcome such a stranger.

She came to us from islands in the West
Because we needed what she had to give –
A two-faced way to welcome such a guest
Who needed just the chance to earn and live.
Such welcome to a stranger!

He came here from a country in the East
To offer us his sorely-needed skill –
On short-term contract only is it leased
Until our needs are met. Does this fulfil
Our welcome to a stranger?

He came from where the ravages of war
Had blown his legs to nothing with a shell,
Launched by an unknown hand without the law
Not caring who was hurt. Did we do well
To welcome such a stranger?

Our privacy is precious; can we face
The prospect that our living-space be shared
With someone from an unknown alien race
Who's fleeing danger? So, are we prepared
To welcome such a stranger?

'For I was hungry and you gave me food,
Relieved the scorching agony of thirst;
You were not too reluctant to intrude
When I was held in chains; in sickness, nursed.
You welcomed such a stranger.'

# Corinthians

The eloquence of angels, without charity
Is but the strident banging of a gong.
The gifts of faith and reason, lacking clarity
Do little to release the world from wrong.
The sacrifice of wealth to feed the poor
Must surely be inspired by love, by charity;
To give one's life, refusing to ignore
The Third World's gasping, desperate disparity.
Patience, kindness, modesty, contentment,
Warm compassion are the signs of charity,
Clear of lies and pride and just resentment,
Friendship melting any insularity.
Love is paramount and, fast entwined
With faith and hope, embraces all mankind.

# *Fruits of the Spirit*

"The very best of these is *love*" –
And surely love
Will lead to holy *joy*.

Joy, the most elusive gift –
A child's delight
And harbinger of *peace*.

The peace of God pervades the heart
With healing touch,
Inspiring *patience* there.

Patience with another's foibles
– And with Time –
Engenders *kindness* too.

Kindness, having once conceived,
Gives joyful birth
To *goodness*, running free.

Goodness wakens full awareness
Of the strength
That *faith* in God provides.

(Cont'd)

True faith will quickly scour away
The crust of pride
Revealing *meekness* too.

Meekness is the golden lamp
To light the way
Towards *control of self.*

Self requires the Spirit's help
To take control –
So filling life with *love.*

(*Galatians 5, 22-23*)

# *Fun*

# Food For Thought

It's fish, they say, that's very good for brains
The phosphorus within ignites all thought
(But check the label where the fish was caught).
So heed the mystic mentor who explains
How vitamins obey the alphabet
And minerals excite the hemispheres,
Dispelling all our morbid fads and fears.
Eat fish lest we forget, lest we forget!
No need to make appointments with the shrink
If fish will keep our grey cells in repair
And shield us from the onset of despair –
If not from that pervasive, fishy stink.
Remember, if that's not your style of food,
'A little of what you fancy does you good.'

# January Vandal

He stalks the roads to spread that film so lethal
And waits to watch the terror,
To hear the squeal of brakes and frantic slither,
The rasp of spinning rubber.

Every pavement he encrusts with subtlety
In hope of broken leg or dislocated hip,
At very least the sprawl of gross indignity,
A graze, a multi-coloured bruise to paint the shin.

With stealth he cracks the pipes within the loft,
Anticipates with glee the final thaw;
So soft, the beat of drip on drip on drip,
The sickening squelch of sodden underlay.

His crackling laughter can be heard beside the frozen pond
As he relaxes his despotic grip just for an instant,
Enticing the unwary skater to display his skill
Then revelling in his victim's panic and his numb discomfort.

His next ambition must be to destroy
The do-good 'fridge – it's there to mar his joy.

# Subtraction

I was never bright at school,
The teacher used to say.
Though as a lad I could quickly add
I could never take away;
So teacher, who was very kind
And knew the skill we lacked,
From time to time
Would repeat this rhyme
To teach us to subtract –

*Oh, you change the sign*
*Of the bottom line*
*And you add, add, add;*
(repeat three times more)

Now I'm an accountant
Who jiggers with figures all day.
Now I'm a dad
I can quickly add;
I can also take away.
So now, the lad who could never sit still
Fidgets with digits in fact
But from time to time
I repeat this rhyme
To remind me to subtract –

*Rhythm and Life*

*Oh, you change the sign*
*Of the bottom line*
*And you add, add, add. . . . . .*

*Composed in Johannesburg at St.Martin's School, Rosettenville*
*some time in the period 1958-63.*

# All Change at Water Loo

I rushed to catch the six-fifteen, quite out of breath;
The lap-top, nestled on my knees,
Would help me solve some enigma of life and death
As frenzied fingers stabbed the keys.
At Waterloo I took the Tube to reach the City,
Jostling all the passers-by;
I reached my desk to cope with all the nitty-gritty,
Frantic calls demanding why
I hadn't sold those risky shares the day before.
Quite late to follow up my hunch
Which now became far too insistent to ignore
My resignation beat the Crunch.

The next few weeks were vacant, glum, as my depression
Deepened, growing ever glummer...
But then, as everyone foresaw a deep recession,
I sought training as a plumber.

Now I bask within the clank of joints and pipes –
The rattle of the Tube was worse! –
Free from all the gloomy cant of City-types,
With time to scribble out a verse.

I really do enjoy the time to fix a junction
(Far, far from Clapham, might I say)
Flushing with success and having no compunction
For keeping heart-attacks at bay.
My simple interest is coping with the pressure
Just the water, not the blood –
The air within the toilet smells distinctly fresher
Now I've stopped that leaking flood.

Having made redundant all those screens and scanners,
I provide employment for my screws and spanners.

# Weedia Ubiquita

My lawn has to cope with an annual menace
As greenness is dotted with *Bellis perennis*
The problem then grows as it widens and deepens
As daisies are joined by *Ranunculus repens*,
While nothing takes note of my total embargo
On any advance by *Plantago virago*;
And if all my vigilance should any laxer come (Ouch, sorry!)
Then all the grass will be swathed in *Taraxicum*.

*Bellis perennis*,
Give me your answer, do;
I'm quite zealous, ridding myself of you.
It won't be a perfect mowing
'Cos you're bound to go on showing,
But you look sweet beneath my feet –
Though just for a day or two.

But troubles with lawns are of very small order
While gaggles of goosegrass are strangling the border;
And whom can I turn to, to act as my saviour
From sneaking incursions of *A. podagravia*?
And if the Ground Elder should teach the Ground Younger,
Then how could we cope with resultant land-hunger?
But almost as bad is the bold *Calystegia*
Whose sinuous tendrils envelope the hedge 'ere. (Ouch, sorry
again)

They seek him here, they seek him there,
But why? He's blooming everywhere.
Those scarlet blooms bear me no malice,
That demmed pervasive *Annagallis*.

And what of the fence where *Clematis alpina*
Is struggling to outsmart *Convolvulus minor* –
While brave *Lonicera* née *periclymenum*
Is fighting with *Tamus* to share space between 'em
And *Hedera helix* is trying to strangle
Dear *Rosa* who's trying to climb through the tangle
And Bindweed attempts to embrace the *Wisteria*
So bringing her near to the verge of hysteria?
Oh, the *Hedera* and the *Ilex!*
When they are both full-grown
Of all the weeds that attack the fence
Ivy surely bears the crown.

**Epilogue**
A cry of distress from the small *Myosotis*,
*"Tell us, o tell us, just how you forgot us!"*

# The Author

Vaughan Stone was born in London and achieved a degree in Forestry at Aberdeen University. His career then led him into teaching – nothing to do with woodlands! first in England, then S. Africa, Iran and Zambia.

The 6 years in S. Africa involved him in serious political writing, mostly satire, including a series in 'Africa South' entitled Grim Fairy Tales.

Abandoning teaching, he embarked on charity work, first with Help the Aged (AgeCare) and then Sue Ryder Foundation (Ryder Care) in their overseas operations (India, Malawi).

After retirement, Vaughan began spending his time on poetry writing. The first collection was published by Green Arrow Publishing under the title 'Life At Large' (ISBN 978-0-9551 431-0-6)

# The Publisher

Green Arrow Publishing is an independent publisher, based in the North-West of England, specialising in the publication of all types of Fiction, Non-fiction, Poetry and Drama. We operate a Collaborative Publishing scheme, providing authors with the opportunity to see their work in print.

We are delighted to have worked with Vaughan Stone on this edition and trust that you will enjoy it as much as we have.

*John Dench*
*Publishing Editor*
*Green Arrow Publishing*